DIGITAL AND INFORMATION LITERACY™

ENHANCING YOUR ACADEMIC DIGITAL FOOTPRINT

NICHOLAS CROCE

rosen publishing's
rosen
central®

New York

Published in 2013 by The Rosen Publishing Group, Inc.
29 East 21st Street, New York, NY 10010

Copyright © 2013 by The Rosen Publishing Group, Inc.

First Edition

Library of Congress Cataloging-in-Publication Data

Croce, Nicholas.
Enhancing your academic digital footprint/Nicholas Croce.
    pages cm.—(Digital and information literacy)
Includes bibliographical references and index.
ISBN 978-1-4488-8355-4 (library binding)—
ISBN 978-1-4488-8362-2 (pbk.)—
ISBN 978-1-4488-8363-9 (6-pack)
1. Résumés (Employment)—Data processing. 2. Career development. 3. Academic achievement. 4. Internet—Safety measures. 5. Reputation. 6. Impression formation (Psychology) I. Title.
HF5383.C755 2013
650.14'2—dc23

2012021988

Manufactured in the United States of America

CPSIA Compliance Information: Batch #W13YA: For further information, contact Rosen Publishing, New York, New York, at 1-800-237-9932.

CONTENTS

INTRODUCTION

Whenever people update a Facebook status, tweet, post to a blog, or tag a photo, they're leaving a digital footprint. These are records of the actions they take online, whether they are through the Web, a smartphone, a tablet, or any other Internet-connected device. A person walking along a beach leaves footprints in the sand. Similarly, wherever a person goes on the Internet, he or she leaves evidence of his or her digital path. Unlike physical footprints, though, a person's digital record doesn't necessarily wash away with time. Photos or other online content can be deleted, of course, but once shared, they can live online forever.

Students today live in a time of great transliteracy, which is the ability to digitally interact across multiple platforms, such as the Web, smartphones, and tablets, and through different services, such as social networks, micro-blogs, and geolocation apps. Advances in technology are also enabling technology companies to store vast amounts of information much more cheaply than ever before. The day will most likely come when virtually all of a person's digital actions will be recorded and stored forever. With this in mind, it's important to understand how your digital footprint can help or harm you. Photos or status updates can live online forever. Images may appear in a search done by a new friend, teacher, or potential employer. Off-putting

An academic digital footprint can benefit students by showcasing their interests and talents online through the use of technologies such as smartphones and tablet computers.

content that a person may have thought he or she deleted can show up where that individual least expected it.

On the other hand, a positive digital footprint can enhance a person's reputation. A favorable online profile showcasing a person's academic achievements can serve as a virtual résumé of her or his life, stressing the individual's drive, intellect, and personality. A young person's academic digital footprint can include presentations of educational interests, such as photos of winning the science fair; a YouTube video of participation in extracurricular activities, like the scoring of a goal at the soccer championship; or displays of volunteer work, like helping at a nursing home. All of the information that appears in an academic digital footprint should give a good impression to anyone who is involved in a student's academic career, whether it be a teacher, coach, possible employer, college recruiter or college admissions officer, or someone considering the student for an internship or volunteer opportunity.

Learning about the tools to use to showcase your academic talents online is crucial. The process is multistaged and can take months, if not years, to accomplish. Once enhanced, your academic digital footprint must be continuously maintained. As technology advances and the Web expands, your academic digital life—and its digital tracks—will grow, too, just like your personal reputation.

Chapter 1

Digital Footprints in the Academic World

According to author and educator William M. Ferriter, "Digital footprints are the trails people leave behind when they live online." The definition of a digital footprint in the academic world is the portfolio of content students create online that represents their educational interests and achievements. For example, a student may express interest in astronomy by publishing a blog on the latest planet discoveries outside the solar system. Although this subject may be a personal hobby, it shows the student's intellectual curiosity and may help him or her academically down the road by catching the eye of a college recruiter or even someone looking to hire the student for a summer internship.

In this sense, a student's personal and academic digital footprints can overlap, but they maintain very important distinctions. A personal footprint also includes content that has nothing to do with school, such as message board comments or journal-style blog postings. However, these personal postings can also become part of one's academic digital footprint because they serve as a window into a student's personality.

File   Edit   View   Favorites   Tools   Help

THERE'S AN APP FOR THAT

There's an App for That

Three Ring is an example of one of the emerging services that uses technology to connect teachers and students. The mission of Three Ring is to "create and share digital portfolios of students' work quickly and easily." Designed as an app, teachers can photograph and upload students' portfolios using their smartphones or tablets. The intent is to collect all of a student's work in one place for easy access by the teacher, who can then pull up the work to look at during a student or parent conference.

What's revolutionary about Three Ring is its ability to give teachers a bird's-eye view of a student's entire body of work in one place. Previously, physical portfolios were difficult for educators to maintain. They were cumbersome and unwieldy, consisting of different types of projects—from writing to artwork. Now, however, educators can have a student's entire academic digital footprint readily available.

Know Who's Searching

Part of being a student is participating in programs that select the best candidates, such as sports teams, internships, and eventually college. Those making the choices about whom to admit to these programs, such as coaches, employers, and college admissions officers, may turn to the Web to find out more about the candidates they wish to select as the best qualified.

Likewise, people may turn to the Web to get a good sense of a person's true personality. A student may enjoy posting pictures of his or her artwork on a photo-sharing site. These postings may give others a good impression of

Today, with nearly everyone having a digital presence, people will use information about you online as a virtual résumé, attempting to find the best applicant for their program.

that student's creativity. Another student may enjoy baking and have unique recipes to share on a personal blog. The baking blog may give people a sense that the individual is not only talented in the kitchen but also passionate about this particular interest.

When doing research, those who type a name into a search engine aren't necessarily spying or trying to dig up negative information on another person. More likely, they're looking for hints of an individual's personality that might not come through elsewhere.

When it comes to online communication, there are clear boundaries being drawn today regarding how students and their teachers can interact. For example, in 2012, the New York City Department of Education released guidelines stating that public school teachers cannot contact students through personal social media pages but can communicate with students through pages that are set up for classroom purposes. New York City's guidelines do not forbid teachers from using social media, but they do require teachers to communicate with students using professional pages devoted to classroom business, such as classroom study guides and homework assignments. Teachers must get official approval from supervisors before creating these pages, though, and parents have to sign a consent form before their kids can participate on these pages.

The guidelines established by New York City's education department are among the first that involve the use of social media in the classroom. They bring to the forefront the issue that interactive technologies are becoming more and more important in students' and teachers' lives and that clear guidelines must be established to prevent any kind of inappropriate contact between students and educators. Administrators also recognize that they have to safeguard the educational benefits of social media as well.

Research Your Footprint

The first step toward enhancing one's academic digital footprint is finding out what it looks like. Most people run a quick search of their name on a popular search engine like Google or Yahoo!, but there's more to it than that. Search engines have grown very sophisticated in how they rank search results. Coders, the computer scientists who create the software behind the search engines, use what are called algorithms. Algorithms are mathematical formulas that calculate a specific outcome. In the case of search engines, the outcome is what search results appear based on the query, who's requesting the search, and where that person is located, among other factors.

"Googling" yourself, or searching for information about yourself online, doesn't mean you're vain. Checking your personal online information helps you determine whether it is accurate or not.

Chapter 2

Understanding the Technology Used in Creating Digital Footprints

Technology advances at an amazing pace. At the turn of the twenty-first century, there were virtually no social networks, smartphones, or apps. Now people wouldn't know what to do without these technologies. This astounding rate of change makes one wonder: what will technology look like ten years from now?

To understand the technologies behind academic digital footprints, it's important to consider what is not yet known about them. There's no telling what the future will be for the information a person uploads to the Web today. It may be used for good or ill, and it has the potential to help, as much as harm, a person's academic reputation. Therefore, it's important to be careful how freely you post content on the Internet. For example, posting untagged photos of yourself pulling a crazy prank after school with friends may seem harmless enough. However, future facial recognition technologies

It's important to understand how technologies such as apps work to make sure you're not unwittingly posting content that might portray you in an unfavorable light.

may make you and your friends identifiable in the images, regardless of whether or not you want to be discovered. Though no one can see into the future and predict what technologies will exist years from now, students can and should fully understand how today's technologies—social media, search engines, and cloud computing—work in creating digital footprints.

File   Edit   View   Favorites   Tools   Help

MOORE'S LAW

Moore's Law

Gordon Moore is a cofounder of Intel, a semiconductor chip manufacturer and one of the largest technology companies in the world. According to Intel's Web site, Moore said, "The number of transistors on a chip will double approximately every two years." This basically means that technological advancement doubles about every two years. In other words, it increases exponentially, or at a rate that grows faster and faster over time.

If the number "1" represents the state of technology today, in two years, it will be "2." Two years later it will reach "4," and then "8" two years after that. After twenty years, that number will have reached 512. In the span of one generation, according to Moore's Law, technology will be 512 times as advanced as it is today.

This illustrates that it's not enough to understand the technology of today. To make smart decisions about how to treat their digital information, students must anticipate how technology will change.

How Social Media Work

A good place to start paying attention to one's digital footprint is social media. Most sites, such as Facebook, Twitter, LinkedIn, Google+, Myspace, and LiveJournal, have one common goal: to collect information on their users. By doing so, they can make money. They collect users' personal information, from account details to what they share with friends. Therefore, social media companies tend to encourage as much sharing as possible, regardless of whether it helps or hurts someone's reputation.

Although social media sites do allow users to keep their personal information concealed with privacy settings, they have been known to encourage

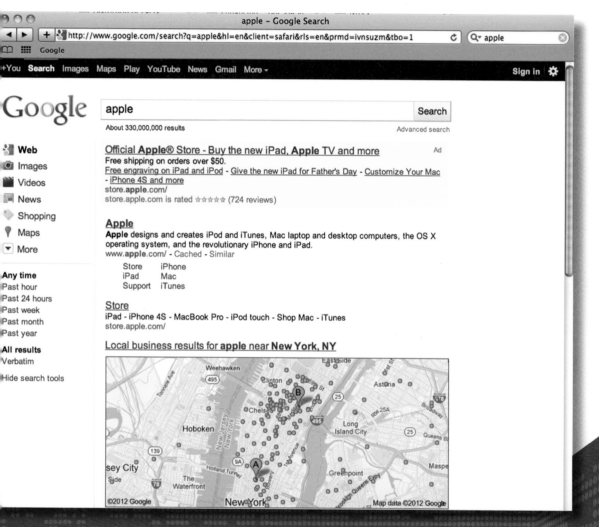

Search engine optimization allows Apple Inc., to be displayed prominently in Google (http://www.google.com) search results for the word "apple."

users to share as much information as possible. Facebook cofounder Mark Zuckerberg has even noted, on his own profile page, "I'm trying to make the world a more open place by helping people connect and share."

How can revealing too much information about oneself hurt? One example is that by not paying attention to a social network's privacy settings one can easily lose track of who is able to see posts on a profile page. A person may have numerous photos posted there, some of which might not portray the individual in the best light, in the eyes of educators, even if the photos are of activities outside of school.

Care should be applied to anything one uploads to social networks, whether it's photos, status updates, comments, likes, follows, check-ins, and so forth. Once the content is in the public space, it may be practically impossible to delete.

People should be particularly careful when tweeting, or posting to Twitter. The microblogging service is designed so that all posts are made public by default. What's more, tweets can easily go viral by being re-tweeted, or relayed by other users. Once someone resends another person's

The Social Media Privacy Act

While there's nothing necessarily wrong with someone searching for academic information about a student, it's never acceptable for anyone, whether a friend, teacher, or employer, to ask for a password to access someone's private accounts to look for information.

In April 2012, the California State Senate passed the Social Media Privacy Act, which bans colleges and employers from asking students, employees, or applicants for username and password access to their social media accounts. Senator Leland Yee, who sponsored the legislation, told the *Los Angeles Times*, "The practice of employers or colleges demanding social media passwords is entirely unnecessary and completely unrelated to someone's performance or abilities."

There will surely be more legislation protecting individual privacy rights as social media profiles increasingly become the go-to place for information on people.

posts, it's virtually out of the control of the creator. Even if that person deletes the post, it may still exist elsewhere on the Web. In addition, Twitter postings are indexed, which means they can show up in search results, making them even more difficult to erase from the Web.

How Search Engines Work

It's widely known that search engines organize the Internet. What's less well understood is just how they do this. It used to be that search engines such as Google, Yahoo!, and Bing, among others, developed their own unique algorithms. These mathematical formulas calculated search results using factors such as how relevant the content was to the query and how popular the Web site was among users. For example, by searching for "apple," the Web site for the technology company Apple Inc., may appear highest in the search ranking because it's the most popular site related to the keyword, even though the searcher may have been looking for information about the fruit. The reason for the highest ranking is because the Apple Inc., Web site is currently more popular than any single site dedicated to the fruit.

The Web site for Apple Inc., is also considered more relevant to the query. The reason is search engine optimization, or SEO. SEO is the science of making Web sites more discoverable through search engines. Computer programmers make Web sites rank higher in search results in a number of ways.

The easiest and most popular strategy is by coding popular search words, called keywords, into the Web site. By strategically coding the keyword "apple" into its site, Apple Inc., convinces search engines that it's the most relevant result of the query.

However, search engines have grown much more sophisticated in recent years, and so has SEO. Not only do search engines factor in the relevance and popularity of sites in their rankings, they also consider one's personal online behavior from search history, biographical information, linked social networks, and more. All of this data is collected through users' personal accounts with the search engine and tracking software called cookies.

Moreover, the distinction between social networks and search engines is quickly fading. Much of what people post to their social network profiles can sneak into search engine results. This fact highlights the importance of not only paying close attention to privacy settings, but also considering carefully what content is uploaded at all.

How Cloud Computing Works

With technology advancing and the price of digital storage decreasing, many businesses are collecting more and more information and storing it for longer than ever. From e-mails to blog posts to photos to account

Cloud computing stores information from your digital devices on outside servers. This convenience comes with the risk of having your content accidentally appear online.

information, most, if not all, of people's digital lives exist on the hardware of corporations.

Commonly known as the "cloud," cloud computing relies on the sharing of computing resources rather than using local servers or personal devices to control the applications. This external storage of data has its benefits and drawbacks, however. One advantage is user convenience. Most cloud services are either inexpensive or free, and they make it easy to upload, download, and store one's data indefinitely. Another plus is sharability. Document-sharing services such as Google Docs, Dropbox, and Apple's iCloud allow students to create and edit content online, access it from any Internet-enabled device, and share it with others. The convenience of cloud computing can be indispensable to students involved in collaborative projects, especially if they're working from different locations.

Another benefit of the cloud is Software as a Service, or SaaS. Instead of downloading expensive software to a computer, a user can simply access the Web-formatted version online for a monthly fee. Adobe Creative Cloud is one example of SaaS. Adobe's visual editing software, including Photoshop for photo editing and InDesign for publication design, can cost hundreds of dollars. Adobe's SaaS program, however, offers these programs online at much cheaper monthly fees, making them affordable for, say, visual arts students who may need them for just a semester.

While the cloud may be convenient and cheap, there's no such thing as a free lunch, as the saying goes. Users may not be paying as much money for these services but they, wittingly or not, may be covering the cost by releasing their personal information and the content they upload. The cloud companies, in turn, use an individual's information to sell advertising.

Chapter 3

Avoiding the Negative

The foundation of a positive academic digital footprint is having respectable online behavior. Students should keep from posting content that can damage their academic reputation among peers and teachers. Ranting blog posts or offensive comments on a social networking profile are just a couple of examples of content that have the potential to stay online indefinitely. The key is to get into the practice of recognizing which content can be harmful and making informed judgments about whether to post it in the first place.

Communicating digitally and communicating in person are vastly different experiences. Up close and personal, one's tone and body language help deliver the meaning behind the message a person wants to convey. Through a screen, however, people lose these nonverbal cues, without which a harmless joke on a status update may come off as an insult. Even if the recipient doesn't find the comment insulting or off-putting, a third-party reader may. What can be an inside joke posted online between two close friends may come off as offensive to outsiders, especially someone of another generation who might have a different sense of humor. When communicating informally with friends, it's often better to do so privately through e-mail or closed messaging rather than in public on the Web.

Because content can live online indefinitely, malicious and unprofessional behavior, such as cyberbullying, can come back to haunt you.

Avoid Unethical Behavior

Harmful behavior such as cyberbullying, sexting, harassment, and trolling shouldn't be practiced or tolerated under any circumstances. Not only can the victims suffer irreparable damage, so, too, can the aggressors when it comes to their online reputations. Just a single incident of any of these behaviors indicates to the academic world that the student has trouble respecting others and likely won't foster a healthy learning environment among his or her peers.

Academic cheating is never acceptable. In the age of social media, it's not only easier than ever to plagiarize or cheat, but it's also easier to get caught.

File   Edit   View   Favorites   Tools   Help

  SPELLING AND GRAMMAR

Spelling and Grammar

In this era of short, quick communication by e-mail, text, or status update, spelling and grammar seem to be growing worse, especially among young people. It's no less important to practice proper English when posting a tweet than when writing a school essay. People are judged by their use of language. Sloppiness often gives others the impression that a person is also careless in other areas of his or her life. Misspellings and poor grammar imply that the writer isn't well educated, even though the opposite may be true.

One of the easiest and most effective ways of enhancing an academic digital footprint is to learn the basic rules of writing. There are great books for students, such as *Grammar Girl Presents the Ultimate Writing Guide for Students* by Mignon Fogarty and the classic *Elements of Style* by William Strunk Jr. and E. B. White, which is available for free online. These guides cover the basics, such as punctuation, sentence structure, and writing clearly. However, the easiest mistakes to correct are spelling. Everyone has access to an online dictionary.

Students commonly sell their term papers online. However, teachers have gotten wise to these schemes and often use software to weed out the cheaters. Even if you don't participate in plagiarism or cheating, be on guard for it. A term paper innocently posted online as part of a résumé or portfolio may be used without the writer's knowledge, implicating the writer even though he or she is innocent.

Deception can do immense damage to a person's academic digital footprint. Discussion or news of cheating can find its way up the search rankings and stay there indefinitely, forever tarnishing a student's reputation. Furthermore, cheating says a lot about a person's ethics, or lack thereof, which carries great weight in educational environments and in future job prospects.

Understand Opinion Etiquette

Young people's opinions grow to define who they are and how they see the world. As technology advances and people's digital identities grow, their digital opinions will come to represent them more and more over time. Therefore, it's important to be fair, reasonable, and professional when

A college athlete displays his Facebook page. Some schools require students to sign an "Internet ethics" policy advising them to be careful about what they put online and warning that school officials will be checking posts.

expressing one's thoughts online, whether it be through e-mail, a profile page, a term paper, a blog posting, a video upload, or a tweet. In particular, when offering your opinion in response to another's, such as commenting on an article, message board, or blog post, try to do so rationally or impartially, without the heated emotion that might drive you to write something that you may regret later.

Strike the Right Balance

Although it's important to be discriminating about what information one shares, it's wise to strike the right balance between what to reveal and what to conceal. If there's a lack of academic information about you on the Web, you run the risk of appearing like you have either nothing to show or something to hide. On the other hand, there's also a risk with oversharing. By inviting people to have access to your academic content, such as term papers, research, and class notes, you increase the chances of that material being used improperly or plagiarized by someone.

MYTHS&FACTS

MYTH A positive academic digital footprint isn't that important for success in school.

FACT Maintaining a positive online academic image is very important for one's educational success. Technology expert Will Richardson describes students' online presence as "portfolios of who we are, what we do, and by association, what we know." Anyone who is looking for information about you will, fairly or not, judge you by your online appearance.

MYTH Anyone can delete anything he or she posts online.

FACT Although someone technically can delete most content posted online, there's virtually no way to erase it from the Internet if it falls into the hands of a third party.

MYTH Students who remain anonymous online don't have to be concerned about their academic digital footprints.

FACT Although no information is better than negative information, being completely anonymous online can make a student appear as if he or she has no accomplishments, interests, or academic pursuits. Anonymity may not hurt an academic reputation, but it probably won't help it either.

Chapter 4

Promoting the Positive

The next strategy for students wanting to enhance their academic digital footprint is to accentuate the positive with a digital makeover. Just as people might dress for success for an important event, such as a presentation or college interview, they can also put on their best online face when it comes to academic achievement. The first step in a digital makeover is for students to take inventory of what information currently exists about them online. Are there old forgotten postings from an online journal? Is there an old Twitter account no longer in use? If so, students should either conceal it through privacy settings or delete the content that doesn't spotlight their academic achievements. Otherwise, the information will compete with the content that does contribute to a positive academic portfolio. A number of ways you can try to clean up unwanted content online include the following:

- Take down blog posts that don't contribute to your academic profile.
- Review your Facebook or other social network sites' privacy settings to ensure that private content isn't publicly visible.
- Thoroughly search for your name to see if there's any overlooked content.

Carefully eliminate objectionable content on blogs, journals, social network sites, and bulletin boards to promote a positive academic digital reputation.

After stripping away the unwanted content, it's time to start creating favorable material. You should start with a focus. If you're interested in science, you should try to concentrate on that particular field. If you're into the performing arts, you might post videos of a recent onstage performance or concert. When building an academic image, the more well defined it is, the stronger the message will be.

Launch an Educational Blog

Educational blogs are an easy and inexpensive way to showcase academic interests and talents. Blogs are also interactive and simple to maintain, which leaves more time for the actual writing. Blogs also allow for multimedia content. In addition to text, one can upload images, audio files, and videos, and add content from other sources to make the work more collaborative and interactive.

First find a subject. If you are interested in physics, you might start to write solely about the science in general. Yet you might want to go further than that. What area of physics? New discoveries? Physics mysteries? Profiles of great minds, such as Albert Einstein, Isaac Newton, and Stephen Hawking? If you are interested in art, you might use the blog's multimedia features to display a painting you created for the school art exhibit. After establishing a niche, a blog can help you stand out and gain a wider audience than just classmates.

Once the focus of the blog is set, it's time to find a platform. There are many free and inexpensive blogging services out there, such as Blogger, WordPress, and Tumblr, among many, many others. Also available are academically oriented blog services such as Edublogs and Kidblog.

After deciding on the focus and platform, it's time to start blogging! Post regularly, once every few days, if possible, and then your readership will come to know the schedule and check in frequently. You should try to make postings informative but fun to keep the readership enthralled and engaged. On this schedule, after a year, the blog might accumulate more than one hundred postings, all of which work to promote your expertise.

Just about anyone can start an educational blog. Most blogging services are free, easy to use, and efficient in helping you promote your academic interests and talents to a wide audience.

Make Use of Online Videos

The video-sharing site YouTube may seem like a place to just view and post lighthearted videos, but it can also be a great tool for promoting one's academic skills. A student may have a talent for the performing arts. Maybe another is an amazing guitar player. Perhaps yet another has a unique talent for gymnastics. Maybe one has a beautiful singing voice. A video on YouTube can show that these people are well rounded with unique interests. Not only might it go "viral," or spread, but it might also rank high among

Making online videos can be as simple or sophisticated as you want. Use a basic camera to record a spot for YouTube or advanced software to produce Webcasts or video blogs.

search results. Moreover, colleges like to get a sense of applicants' personalities when reviewing prospects. A video can communicate much more about someone's interests than an application form can.

Another use for online video is digital storytelling. As the name implies, digital storytelling is telling stories through digital media. The advantages of using video, however, include being able to use not only text and audio narration, but images and music as well.

Digital storytelling topics are abundant. They can range from a particular subject, such as history, or a favorite hobby. The video length can be anywhere

‐ ☐ X

le   Edit   View   Favorites   Tools   Help

   VIRTUAL BOOKSHELVES

Virtual Bookshelves

Reading was once a solitary activity, but that's no longer always the case. So-called social reading sites, or social book clubs, allow people to share what they are reading with others. They can see what books their friends or followers of their profile recommend, as well as share comments and reviews.

Some of the most popular sites today include Goodreads, LibraryThing, Copia, Shelfari, Scribd, and BookGlutton. Each site is unique in the services that it offers. Some allow users to link to a person's Amazon book purchases or, like LibraryThing, help catalog book purchases. (Shelfari is owned by Amazon.) Goodreads gives readers suggestions of books to read that are similar to their favorites. BookGlutton enables friends, writers, and students to study and discuss specific texts online. In addition, teachers can provide content questions to particular paragraphs to help their students in examining works that are being discussed in the classroom.

How can this help one's academic digital footprint? Many of these sites offer social networking apps, which allow users to display what they are reading on their profile pages. A virtual bookshelf can be a great way to easily display one's interests because it can show up in a search for your name by anyone looking for information on your interests.

from two to ten minutes, and the video can be a great tool for exposing viewers to a tale they had not heard previously.

One video service that focuses on academics is SchoolTube. Like YouTube, SchoolTube allows students and teachers to post and share. The one difference is that it's educational material. Although YouTube may be more popular and give a student greater exposure, a smaller niche site like SchoolTube can offer a more focused audience for learning and instruction.

Share Academic Experiences

Blogs are just one way to share academic interests with the world. Social platforms such as social networks (for example, Edmodo, Students Circle Network, Facebook, or Google+), photo-sharing sites (Picasa, Pinterest), and wikis (Wikispaces) enable students to post and share different types of content online.

With educational social networks, such as Edmondo and Students Circle Network, you can create something akin to a Facebook profile for your academic interests. Social networks are powerful tools for education because students can collaborate with teachers and peers, even those they may not know personally, and share a knowledge base. There are also endless widgets available, such as surveys, calendars, and more, that can help young people not only teach, but also learn from others through the collaborative use of these tools.

You may want to turn to photo-sharing sites if your academic interests lend themselves to visual content. You can use the more popular services such as Flickr, Photobucket, Snapfish, and Picasa. To keep the focus on education, you just need to create a folder titled, for instance, "Woodworking Projects," "My Winning Touchdowns," "Scenes from My School Play," or "Photojournalism Portfolio." Many of these photo- and video-sharing services offer apps that let anyone with a smartphone upload photos and videos easily and instantaneously.

For a more interactive experience, wikis may be the place to go. These platforms allow for collaborative creating and editing of content. Wikipedia is the best-known wiki, which is designed as an encyclopedia. However, wikis can be about anything. The popular service Wikispaces can host a subject-specific wiki. Contributors can upload text and multimedia, making the topic much more rich and dynamic than if it were just maintained by a single user.

TEN GREAT QUESTIONS
TO ASK A COMPUTER EXPERT

1   Are there social networking services available that are specifically geared toward students?

2   How can I get someone to take down information that's unflattering to me?

3   What apps are available that I can use for academic research?

4   How can I make sure Web sites aren't collecting my personal information?

5   How can I make my content rank high among search results?

6   What is search engine optimization, and how can I use it to my academic digital footprint's advantage?

7   How can I recover from a damaged academic digital footprint?

8   Are there software programs to help me enhance my online academic reputation?

9   How can I protect my online content from plagiarism or theft?

10   What are easy and affordable ways to build a professional-looking Web site?

Chapter 5

Maintaining One's Academic Reputation Online

Enhancing an academic digital footprint is an ongoing process, much like tending to a garden. Profiles need to be updated. Negative information needs to be reviewed and deleted. Most important, however, new content needs to be created, not only to keep information up to date, but also to continue to grow one's digital reach.

Publish or Perish

"Publish or perish" is a phrase used among academics that stresses the importance of regularly writing and publishing papers and books to build a career. Today, the same goes for students, but in a different way. In this age of convenient, frictionless electronic publishing, it's much easier for anyone to have an article appear in an online magazine, journal, or blog,

Blogging can be as easy as telling the world about your hobby or as involved as reporting breaking news as a citizen journalist. This student is recording the sounds of conflict between police and protesters outside a university campus.

or for people to publish their own books. These writing credentials not only expand one's footprint, but they may also appear high in search engine rankings.

As with all areas of building an academic reputation, you should continue to focus on a specific interest or skill. Within that interest, however, it's good to build a niche, a focus within that subject that no one has yet addressed. The more pinpointed the area of expertise, the easier it is for you to make yourself known.

You should also maintain a dedicated blog. This will continue to build readership and serve as a base from which to start publishing elsewhere, such as edited journals and even books. Check out national teen online magazines such as Teen Ink, which includes teen writing, art, photos, and forums, or Frodo's Notebook, an independent magazine for teens who take writing seriously. There are sites such as Student Publishing and Studentreasures that are designed for young people looking to publish their academic material in book form. Other self-publishing services for the general public include Lulu, Blurb, and iUniverse, which can format content as a physical or electronic book to be sold online.

As a credential, however, the strongest is publication in an online, peer-reviewed journal. Once students have a number of writing samples in hand, they can start sending material to editors of respected publications.

In California, these young writers meet Curt Lowens *(seated)*, a Holocaust survivor. The teens are competing in Chapman University's annual Holocaust Art and Writing Contest for middle and high school students, which features essays, poems, or artwork about Holocaust survivors.

Although it's always difficult to get published, there are few better credits than having one's name in a widely read publication.

Enroll in Writing Contests

Online writing competitions can be valuable credentials to add to one's academic profile. There are countless contests held by organizations in all areas, ranging from art to engineering. One example is a contest held by the charity arm of the Holland & Knight law firm. The Holocaust Remembrance Project awards $250 to $5,000 for the best essays that, according to its Web site, "analyze why it is vital that the remembrance, history and lessons of the Holocaust be passed to new generations; and suggest what you, as students, can do to combat and prevent prejudice, discrimination and violence in our world today."

The Scholastic Art & Writing Awards strive to shine a national spotlight on young people with exceptional artistic and literary talent. Past winners of the awards include the artist Andy Warhol and writers Sylvia Plath, Truman Capote, and Joyce Carol Oates, among other notables. Winners can be awarded scholarships, exhibitions of their work in galleries across the nation, and publication of writings in the *National Catalog*, *Best Teen Writing*, and *Spark*, which are distributed to schools and libraries across the country.

Schedule Routine Maintenance

While continuing to create content, it's also essential to run routine checks on how that material shows up in search results. Schedule a weekly or monthly review. Search engines update their algorithms frequently, sometimes even several times a day, to keep their results fresh and relevant. This updating can change the search results that appear for any particular query, including that for a student's credentials. If a blog post appeared first in a search for one's name, it may fall to second, third, or tenth the next time the same search query is run. With routine maintenance, students can make sure their

File   Edit   View   Favorites   Tools   Help

AUTOMATIC ALERTS

Automatic Alerts

In addition to running scheduled checkups on an academic digital footprint, you can use technology to do some of the work. Services such as Google Alerts and Reputation.com enable users to monitor the Web and receive an alert when specific words or phrases appear online, such as "jane smith" or "tim jones chemistry experiments."

With Google Alerts, individuals can request that they receive an e-mail when any such combination of words appears in a blog post, news article, or elsewhere on the Web. This is an easy way to instantaneously know if content that can help or hurt a reputation appears online. Reputation.com is even more comprehensive. As a paid service, it offers a range of products that not only monitor the Web but also work to protect a person's privacy and enhance that person's digital reputation.

information is displayed in the most favorable way. A blog post or personal Web page can be retitled to more accurately describe its content, for example. Otherwise, deleting nonacademic content may push one's more positive material higher in the search rankings.

Create Great Content

The most effective way to create and maintain a positive academic digital footprint is simple: do great work. Creating quality content, such as writing insightful blog posts or sharing valuable research on a specific subject, engages one's audience and strengthens an academic reputation.

These high school students have created an online school newspaper and are getting guidance on the layout from a teacher. You can enhance your academic digital footprint by concentrating on the subjects that excite you. Your skills will strengthen your academic reputation online.

There are several ways to enhance quality. The first is to have a clear message. Students should try to focus on one or two subject areas that interest them, such as chemistry or dance. This makes it easy for a student to build a reputation for being an expert in that field. It also shows others, such as educators or college admissions boards, that this person has a clear focus and exhibits discipline and drive.

Another way to enhance content quality is to follow the standards of traditional academic research. Just because it's a blog post instead of a term paper doesn't mean that the writer can skip doing the research. You should always use reliable sources such as peer-reviewed encyclopedias, books, newspapers, and other edited material, not user-generated content such as other blog posts, message boards, or wikis. Students should also make sure their content looks professional, as if it were being put into print, with flawless grammar and spelling. This practice should apply to all platforms, whether it's an essay, blog, or status update.

Above all, be passionate about your online work. By writing about an area that you love and have a genuine enthusiasm for, your academic footprint will be a positive reflection of yourself and present the best impression in a digital world.

algorithm A mathematical formula designed to produce a specific outcome.

app Short for "application"; a type of software used on mobile devices such as smartphones and tablets.

cloud computing A type of data storage in which an individual's personal content is stored on third-party servers.

content Any type of media, including documents, photos, videos, audio files, etc., that is usually stored online.

cyberbullying The act of bullying over any digital device, such as a computer, phone, or smartphone.

etiquette Appropriate behavior practiced in a particular environment.

extracurricular Relating to programs and activities, such as sports, that are practiced outside of school.

geolocation A capability of an app on a connected device that determines the location of the user.

microblog A blog that allows for short-form posts, such as Twitter and Tumblr.

peer-reviewed Describes a publication that is vetted by professionals in the field.

plagiarism The act of stealing another's writing and using it as one's own.

sexting Sending sexual messages or images over text message.

tablet A type of computer, such as an iPad, used for consuming media rather than content creation.

tagging The act of linking one's social network profile to online photos.

trolling Sending inflammatory digital messages with the intent of inciting an angry response.

tweet A message sent through the microblogging service Twitter.

wiki A Web site that allows for collaborative content creation and editing.

FOR MORE INFORMATION

Canadian Intellectual Property Office
CIPO Client Service Centre
Place du Portage I
50 Victoria Street, Room C-229
Gatineau, QC K1A 0C9
Canada
(866) 997-1936
Web site: http://www.cipo.ic.gc.ca
The Canadian Intellectual Property Office is the official government agency in
    Canada that deals with copyright law and intellectual property issues.

Copyright.gov
Library of Congress
Copyright Office
101 Independence Avenue SE
Washington, DC 20559-6000
Web site: http://www.copyright.gov
Copyright.gov is the Web site for the U.S. Copyright Office, which offers
    information on American copyright law.

Making It Count
Monster.com
8280 Greensboro Drive, Suite 900
McLean, VA 22102
(877) 668-1188
Web site: http://www.makingitcount.com
Making It Count is a program sponsored by Monster.com, offering students
    information on how to transition out of college to higher education or
    into a career.

Office of the Privacy Commissioner of Canada
112 Kent Street, Place de Ville
Tower B, 3rd Floor
Ottawa, ON K1A 1H3
Canada
(613) 947-1698
Web site: http://www.priv.gc.ca
This government office advocates privacy rights for Canadians and looks
    into complaints about privacy violations.

Reputation.com
1001 Marshall Street, 2nd Floor
Redwood City, CA 94063
(650) 241-7491
Web site: http://www.reputation.com
Reputation.com's mission is to protect and enhance the online reputations of
    its subscribers.

Web Sites

Due to the changing nature of Internet links, Rosen Publishing has developed
an online list of Web sites related to the subject of this book. This site is
updated regularly. Please use this link to access the list:

http://www.rosenlinks.com/DIL/ADig

FOR FURTHER READING

Andrews, Lori B. *I Know Who You Are and I Saw What You Did: Social Networks and the Death of Privacy*. New York, NY: Free Press, 2012.

Auletta, Ken. *Googled: The End of the World as We Know It*. New York, NY: Penguin, 2009.

Bauerlein, Mark. *The Digital Divide: Arguments for and Against Facebook, Google, Texting, and the Age of Social Networking*. New York, NY: Jeremy P. Tarcher/Penguin, 2011.

Dover, Danny. *Search Engine Optimization Secrets*. Hoboken, NJ: Wiley, 2010.

Frith, Jordan. *Mobile Interfaces in Public Spaces: Locational Privacy, Control, and Urban Sociability*. New York, NY: Routledge, 2012.

Handley, Ann, and C. C. Chapman. *Content Rules: How to Create Killer Blogs, Podcasts, Videos, Ebooks, Webinars (and More) That Engage Customers and Ignite Your Business*. Hoboken, NJ: Wiley, 2011.

Ivester, Matt. *Lol—Omg!: What Every Student Needs to Know About Online Reputation Management, Digital Citizenship, and Cyberbullying*. Reno, NV: Serra Knight, 2011.

Levmore, Saul X., and Martha Craven Nussbaum. *The Offensive Internet: Speech, Privacy, and Reputation*. Cambridge, MA: Harvard UP, 2012.

Rosen, Jeffrey, and Benjamin Wittes. *Constitution 3.0: Freedom and Technological Change*. Washington, DC: Brookings Institution, 2011.

Rowse, Darren, and Chris Garrett. *Problogger: Secrets for Blogging Your Way to a Six-Figure Income*. Hoboken, NJ: Wiley, 2012.

Safko, Lon. *The Social Media Bible: Tactics, Tools, and Strategies for Business Success*. Hoboken, NJ: Wiley, 2010.

Solove, Daniel J. *Nothing to Hide: The False Tradeoff Between Privacy and Security*. New Haven, CT: Yale University Press, 2011.

Turkle, Sherry. *Alone Together: Sociable Robots, Digitized Friends, and the Reinvention of Intimacy and Solitude*. New York, NY: Basic, 2011.

Bits Blog. "Daily Report: New York City Sets Social Media Rules for Teachers." *New York Times*. Retrieved May 2, 2012 (http://bits. blogs.nytimes.com/2012/05/02/daily-report-new-york-city-sets-social-media-rules-for-teachers).

Campbell, Susan. "Five Online Reputation Management Tips for Students." Reputation.com. Retrieved April 25, 2012 (http://www.reputation. com/reputationwatch/articles/five-online-reputation-management-tips-students).

Ferriter, William M. "Positive Digital Footprints." *Educational Leadership*, April 2011. Retrieved April 26, 2012 (http://www.ascd.org/ publications/educational-leadership/apr11/vol68/num07/Positive-Digital-Footprints.aspx).

Intel.com. "Moore's Law Inspires Intel Innovation." Retrieved April 25, 2012 (http://www.intel.com/content/www/us/en/silicon-innovations/ moores-law-technology.html).

Oricchio, Renee. "Mark Zuckerberg's Privacy Settings." Inc.com. Retrieved April 25, 2012 (http://www.inc.com/tech-blog/mark-zuckerbergs-privacy-settings.html).

Richardson, W. "Footprints in the Digital Age." *Educational Leadership*, November 2008. Retrieved April 26, 2012 (http://www.ascd.org/ publications/educational-leadership/nov08/vol66/num03/Footprints-in-the-Digital-Age.aspx).

Valenza, Joyce. "On Transliteracy: Learning More." *School Library Journal*, May 9, 2010. Retrieved April 25, 2012 (http://blog. schoollibraryjournal.com/neverendingsearch/2010/05/09/ on-transliteracy-learning-more).

Wikispaces. "Springfield Library." Retrieved May 3, 2012 (http:// springfieldlibrary.wikispaces.com).

INDEX

About the Author

Nicholas Croce is the author of *Detectives: Life Investigating Crime, Newton and the Three Laws of Motion*, and *Cool Careers Without College for People Who Love Video Games*. In addition to his experience writing for young adults, he has done consulting work with Internet technology company Seecast Media. He lives in New Jersey.

Photo Credits

Cover and p. 1 (left) © iStockphoto.com/nullplus; cover and p. 1 (middle left) © iStockphoto.com/Huchen Lu; cover and p. 1 (middle right), p. 13 © iStockphoto.com/LdF; cover and p. 1 (right) © iStockphoto.com/Slobodan Vasic; p. 5 Peter Dazeley/Photographer's Choice/Getty Images; p. 9 Mike Powell/Digital Vision/Getty Images; p. 11 Jack Hollingsworth/Photodisc/Thinkstock; p. 18 iStockphoto/Thinkstock; p. 21 Eyecandy Images/Thinkstock; pp. 23, 29, 39 © AP Images; p. 27 BananaStock/Thinkstock; p. 30 © Rodger Mallison/MCT/Landov; p. 35 Jason Andrew/Getty Images; p. 36 © Ana Venegas/The Orange County Register/ZUMA Press; cover (background) and interior page graphics © iStockphoto.com/suprun.

Designer: Nicole Russo; Photo Researcher: Amy Feinberg